HISTORIC ANS'

PEOPLE &

CW00919853

First published 1999
Copyright of the Kilrenny & Anstruther Burgh Collection
ISBN 0 9536538 0 3

Edited by Stephanie Stevenson
Contributors - Wilma Anderson, Margaret Darwood, John Dishman,
Dibbie Greig, Peter & Masry Prince, Alex Rodger and Stephanie Stevenson
Illustrations by Margaret Darwood, Masry Prince and William Stevenson
Map drawn by Richard Ellison

In 1980 the Anstruther Improvement Association organised a Triple Town Exhibition to show archives, photographs and significant items associated with the Royal Burgh of Kilrenny, Anstruther Easter & Wester. It was felt that this exhibition should be retained and enlarged, and eventually a home was found in the Scottish Fisheries Museum. Later, as the Museum developed, more space was required to house fishing artefacts. The A.I.A. felt unable to manage and store the archives. To resolve this crisis a public meeting was called by Elizabeth Gordon, President of the A.I.A. and Murray Anderson, Chairman of the Community Council. As a result the Burgh Collection was formed under the chairmanship of Alex Darwood. Currently the archives are housed in the Murray Library, where the work of collecting and clarifying material continues.

The Burgh Collection are grateful for a grant from the Dalziel Trust to publish a booklet on Historic Anstruther. This is the first in what it is hoped will be a series of publications on different aspects of the histories of Kilrenny, Cellardyke & Anstruther.

Published by Kilrenny & Anstruther Burgh Collection
David Murray Library, Shore Street, Anstruther, Fife KY10
Website at http:/freespace.virgin.net/anstruther.collection
Email to anstruther.collection@virgin.net
Telephone: 01333 311991

Printed by Levenmouth Printers, Buckhaven, Fife KY8 1JH

CONTENTS

There is street map of Anstruther & Cellardyke between pages 16 & 17.
It has numbered references to the houses described in this booklet.

PREFACE

Anstruther is a very ancient settlement area. A red granite axe was found near the Cellardyke bathing pool in 1938 and another prehistoric tool was found near the Marches in 1956. If the tools belonged to the places where they were found they indicate ancient settlements and an ancient trade as no red granite occurs in Fife.

The Romans, when they came north of the Forth estuary in the first century A D, found a painted people and the description *picti* or painted came to be used as the name of the people. Some of these Picts had doubtless been attracted to this area by the sheltered site, the sandy foreshore and the many streams and springs of fresh water.

Christianity was brought to the east coast Picts in the early fifth century. The names of both Anstruther and Kilrenny probably derive from a Celtic saint Ethernan, who died in 699 A D "among the Picts". A chapel was dedicated to him at Kilrenny, anciently Kilretheni, *kil* or chapel of Ethernan. In a Royal Charter of the sixteenth century Anstruther appears as Athernynstruther - Ethernan's streams, from the Gaelic *sruth* or *sruthair*, meaning stream or place of streams, of which Anstruther has many .

In early times the higher parts of Fife were moorland and forest; in the fertile coastal lands oats, bere or barley, beans and wheat were cultivated and cattle kept for milk. By the sixteenth century the regular fishing of herring and white fish was established and there was a profitable trade in fish, grain, hides, salt and some coal from the Fife ports to England, the Low Countries, the Baltic and France. Salmon fishing also flourished.

Anstruther had been a fishing haven since at least the twelfth century when harbour and fishing dues were granted to the monks of May by William I, grandson of the founder of the monastery, David I. Fish curing, coopering, boat building, net-making and later the manufacture of oilskins and canvas floats provided local employment. The 1855 census shows that 2,295 people in the Anstruther burghs were employed in fishing and ancillary industries.

Then there were the occupations supporting the community: baking, brewing, butchery weaving, tailoring, tanning and shoemaking. By the end of the nineteenth century there were three primary schools and one secondary school, five churches of different denominations, a resident doctor and a veterinary surgeon. Each of the three burghs, East Anstruther, West Anstruther and Kilrenny, that make up the present Anstruther, had until 1929 its own harbour (Kilrenny's harbour was in Nether Kilrenny, now Cellardyke, but more properly Sillerdyke from the profusion of silver fish scales on the rocks and streets) and its own independent Town Council.

The picture that emerges is of a busy, largely self-supporting community. Significantly the employers, the merchants, sea captains and professionals, all chose to live within the burghs. The larger houses still standing testify to the way all classes lived closely together.

In the first of what we hope will be a series on different historical aspects of the united burgh we have focused on some of the interesting individuals who have lived here and the buildings associated with them. There are some omissions, subjects which will be covered in later publications that we are planning.

We are indebted to Dr Stephanie Stevenson for much of the material in this book and for her supervision of the research.Thanks also to William Stevenson for many of the line drawings, to the volunteers who wrote up and put together the entries, to John Dishman who typed it all on to disc, and to Patrick Rentoul of PR Print & Design, Cupar who provided helpful advice on the reproduction of the pictures for this booklet.

All research owes much to the efforts of previous writers and this booklet is no exception. We have listed our references at the back and recommend them to those who want to delve further into the burgh's history.

The Chalmers' Memorial Church was an Anstruther landmark for a hundred years. Demolition followed a fire in 1992.

2 **Chalmers' Memorial Church**

THE FISHER LASS / 1

The image of a fisher lass which greets us on notices around the East Neuk of Fife is based on an oil painting by John M. McGhie, the *Sma' Lines*, which shows a woman carrying a basket of fish which would have been caught on the sma' lines she herself would have baited.

There is another famous painting by the same artist in the Fisheries Museum, *The Fisher Lass*. It hung for many years in the front window of John Martin's oilskin factory in East Forth Street, Cellardyke, when William Carstairs owned and managed the factory. Provost Carstairs, who died in 1952, had a fine collection of pictures and memorabilia which he left to the then Town Council of Anstruther and which eventually became the nucleus of the Scottish Fisheries Museum.

The subject of the picture, Jessie Hughes, was brought up in a house at the Gyles, Pittenweem. She married Thomas Russell. After her husband's death she emigrated with her son to Australia, where she died in 1976. Her ashes were returned to Scotland to be buried with her husband.

John M. McGhie (1867-1952) was born in Glasgow. He studied at the Glasgow School of Art, the Royal Academy Schools, and the Academie Julien, Paris. A painter and etcher of coastal scenes, in later years he spent his summers at his studio in Pittenweem. He exhibited at the Royal Academy, the Royal Scottish Academy , the Royal Scottish Society of Watercolour Artists, and the Glasgow Institute. His work can be seen in Glasgow and Paisley Art Galleries.

Women were important workers in the fishing industry, gathering bait, mending nets and cleaning and preparing fish which was sent to Edinburgh, Glasgow, London and to the continent as far as Germany and Russia. It was considered a poor bargain to marry a girl from outside the fishing community because she would not be trained to this necessary work.

Alexander Rodger, sea captain and shipowner, was born in November 1801 at 26 Shore Street, Cellardyke. He was educated at the Parish School in East Forth Street and passed the first 19 years of his life in his native village. At the fishing and by studying hard he acquired a knowledge of navigation which was unusual for someone of his age and limited opportunities.

At the age of about 19 he joined a collier as a sailor and in little more than a year was appointed second mate, being promoted two years later to the command of a brig in which he made many successful voyages to the Mediterranean. He subsequently sailed over the world and was the commander of the first ship of any size or tonnage to sail from Glasgow to an Australian port.

An incident that well illustrates his character occurred when he was making a voyage in his own ship, the *Helen*, through the Indian seas, when drifting with little or no wind but with a heavy swell, the ship struck a sunken reef where according to the charts there was a clear and open sea. The violence of the shock made the ship quiver from stem to stern and a large piece of her false keel was knocked away and floated alongside. Once clear of the reef it was ascertained that the pumps could keep the water from gaining a hold so Captain Rodger lowered a boat and made the most careful soundings and bearings of the reef. On his return home he reported the results to the Admiralty. 'Rodger's Rock' was thereafter recorded on the chart.

After years of hard service Captain Rodger was compelled by failing health to retire from the sea and it was about this time that the first news of the Australian goldfields reached this country. He immediately planned an expedition to the goldfields, which he led himself, consisting of sixteen young fishermen from Cellardyke, five of whom were his own nephews. After spending six months with the expedition, the success of which can be gathered from the fact that the £1,200 advanced towards the expedition was repaid and each member had about £200 over, he returned home.

He then began another speculative enterprise. He had long been convinced that fast clipper ships had great advantages in the China tea trade and by 1855 he was part owner of the *Kate Carnie* with C. Carnie of Glasgow. This was the first clipper ship built by Steele & Co. Next came the *Ellen Rodger*, named after his wife, with Captain John Keay of Anstruther as her master. Next came *Min*, Captain John Smith, Anstruther, and in 1863 his most famous clipper *Taeping*, which in 1866 won the most exciting tea race of them all.

Taeping, Captain McKinnon, drawing less water than *Ariel* tied up in London docks twenty minutes ahead of Captain Keay, 99 days out of Foochow. Such a close and exciting finish had never been seen before in an ocean race. *Taeping* divided her winnings of 10 shillings per ton with the crew of the *Ariel* and Captain McKinnon divided the captain's £100 with Captain Keay.

Taeping

Local interest in the race was intense as *Ariel* was captained by Captain Keay of Anstruther and included Anster men in her crew while *Taeping* was owned by Captain Rodger of Cellardyke and her crew included Dykers. His last clipper ship, the *Lahloo* , was built in 1867.

When *Lahloo* and *Taeping* were both lost in the East in 1872 he sold the *Min* and retired. He bought a field at the east end of Cellardyke for the use of the community and had rocks cleared from the harbour entrance and each winter he gave £20 for the poor of the burgh. For many years he was an examiner for marine certificates and served on the board of Clyde Lighthouses. He died on June 6th 1877 at Newton Place, Glasgow, after a short illness in his 76th year. Rodger Street, Cellardyke, was named after him.

Very little is known about Captain John Smith, who was born in 1824 in a house in East Green. His father had been a captain of a vessel which went to the Greenland whale fishing, but when that enterprise died out he bought a large sloop and was engaged for some time in the coasting trade. His son accompanied him in the sloop and at the age of 14 began his professional career in the *Jessie* of Anstruther.

15 East Green

John Smith made his reputation in two of Captain Rodger's tea clippers. Basil Lubbock in his book *The China Clippers* writes that John Smith was "one of those daring skippers who carried sail and was not afraid of a reef-studded passage". And again:

> . . there are a few men, who held the necessary qualifications of a tea-ship commander, whose endurance equalled their energy, whose daring was tempered by good judgment, whose business capabilities were on a par with their seamanship and whose nerves were of cast iron. Amongst the best known were Robinson of *Sir Lancelot*, Keay of *Ariel*, McKinnon of *Taeping*, Shewan of *Norman Court*, Burgoyne of *Titania*, John Smith of *Lahloo* and Orchard of *Lothair*.

Of these eight captains, two came from Anstruther, both proteges of Captain Rodger. Captain Smith captained the second of Rodger's ships, the *Min*, in 1862 and served in it until Rodger had the *Lahloo* built in 1867 when he was her master as long as Rodger owned her. ·

After the loss of the *Lahloo* Smith was offered command of the iron ship the *Maju* of which he was part owner. She left Dundee on her maiden voyage in October 1874 with coals for Rangoon. The pilot was landed when they reached the Pentland Firth. Intelligence from Stornaway reported that on Wednesday 21st October a large 3-masted vessel was seen in the Atlantic about 12 miles off Barvas, Isle of Lewis.There was a tremendous sea and she appeared quite helpless being driven towards the coast. That night the gale increased and next morning no vessel was to be seen.

· That afternoon large quantities of wreckage were found on the beach at Barvas including a piece of boat's stern with *Maju London* in black letters on the stern.The captain and the entire crew were lost. Captain Smith was about 51 years of age. He left a widow and three children and was buried near his home in Riccarton, Kilmarnock.

Dundee was to have been the ship's home port and Captain Smith seems to have planned to return with his family to his native town, having bought a new house, *High Cross*, on Pittenweem Road - now the guest house, *The Spindrift*. A small room at the top of the house with an unobstructed view of the harbour was made to resemble a ship's cabin; lined with wood it once had a bunk bed, a ship's stove, mahogany shelves and brass fittings.

Archibald Johnston, son of Andrew Johnston, merchant and baillie in Anstruther Easter married in 1820 Mary Clarkson, heiress of John Clarkson, Senior Baxter Burgess in Edinburgh. He owned a seventeenth century house in a close behind Shore Street with a large garden which extended to the Back Dykes. In 1828 Johnston demolished the old house and built a new villa in the garden on the raised beach to the east of the old manse. It was built in a style typical of the period and of the district, flat-fronted, a large window on either side of a central door, three similar windows on the first floor, two attics and a semi-basement.

Archibald Johnston and Mary Clarkson lived in St Andrews where Johnston was Agent for the Bank of Scotland. After he died in 1829 at the age of forty four the new villa was rented to tenants until 1852 when George Darsie tanner, and his wife, Margaret Johnston Walker (a cousin perhaps of Archibald Johnston) bought it for £690 sterling.

Johnston Lodge

George Darsie, a public-spirited man, was the eldest son of George Darsie, several times first baillie of Anstruther Easter. The tannery was on the north side of East Green below the Old Police House until it was destroyed by fire in 1906. Darsie's descendants and connections occupied Johnston Lodge for just over a hundred years.

Four of Darsie's sons left Anstruther as young men, three of them for Pittsburgh, Pennsylvania, and the eldest of them, George, for Liverpool probably to join the trading firm of Balfour Williamson set up there in 1851.

The following year the firm opened a trading station in Valparaiso, Chile, the first Europeans to do so. After a few years there George moved to Tahiti to join the trading firm of John Brander from Elgin who had contacts with Balfour Williamson in the Pacific.

John Brander made a considerable fortune in Tahiti developing his large estates and trading in pearls, mother of pearl and copra with his own fleet of sailing vessels. In 1856 he married the young *Tetuanui i reia i te Raiatea*, known as Titaua Marama, eldest daughter of the chiefess Arriitaimai and an English trader, Alexander Salmon, who had arrived in the islands in 1841. The princess and her brothers and sisters were all sent away to school, some to Sydney, some to Valparaiso and others to an aunt in the south of England. The American historian, Henry Adams, who met the adult princess said that she spoke excellent English and was familiar with America and Europe. She and John Brander had nine children and at least two of the five boys were educated at Madras College in St Andrews.

Princess Titaua Marama was widowed in 1875 and a week after her husband's death she announced that she would continue the business of her late husband in all its branches, which she did for sixteen years, and that she would sign herself *T. Salmon, Widow Brander*. She was an intelligent, business-like woman and she loved giving parties, having plenty of opportunity for doing so. As "first lady"of Tahiti, taking the place of her sister, Marau, who had divorced the alcoholic king, Pomare V, she entertained all important visitors to the island, English and French, including Queen Victoria's son, Alfred, Duke of Edinburgh, whom she entertained lavishly at Papeete during his tour of the Pacific in 1868.

In 1878, at the age of thirty six, Princess Titaua Marama married her manager, George Darsie, a year older than herself. They had three children, Georgina, George and Lieumonte, all born in Tahiti. At the age of fifty Darsie retired with his family to Johnston Lodge bringing with him Titaua's two youngest Brander daughters and John the cook. The princess was not unfamiliar with the Scottish climate as she and John Brander had made at least one visit to Scotland, to Elgin in 1865.

After only six years in Johnston Lodge the princess died in her fifty sixth year. She was buried in the parish churchyard and is commemorated on a pink granite tombstone on the south side of the church.

Johnston Lodge assumed its present appearance in 1912 a year after Georgina Darsie married Thomas Murray, solicitor son of the manse next door. Like her mother Georgina loved giving parties so she and, her husband had a ballroom built on the east gable of the house, together with a new entrance gate in Hadfoot Wynd and a porch, all harmoniously in keeping with the 1828 house. The architects were Gillespie & Scott of St Andrews.

Unfortunately Georgina was rather too generous and extravagant and in 1926, three years after the death of her husband, she was declared bankrupt. Her half-sister, Paloma Brander with her husband the Revd Andrew MacLachlan whom she had married in 1900 when he was minister at the United Presbyterian Church in the Back Dykes (now the Erskine Hall), bought the house and lived in it for the next thirty years. Paloma died in 1955 and Andrew MacLachlan died in 1957. The house remained empty for fourteen years, gathering brambles in the basement and a reputation for being haunted by a Green Lady.

Finally in 1970 a young surveyor in Edinburgh bought the coach house, formerly the granary of an eighteenth century malt steading which Archibald Johnston had bought in 1819, for conversion into two holiday homes and he was largely responsible for interesting the National Trust of Scotland in the restoration of Johnston Lodge. By 1973 the Trust had successfully converted the sadly neglected building into three self contained, freehold flats.

John Goodsir (1814-1867) was born in Anstruther and brought up in the Hermitage. There is a plaque to commemorate him on the house, which is situated at the end of Back Dykes, just above School Green.

The Hermitage

John Goodsir studied at St Andrews and Edinburgh universities, then practised medicine with his father in Anstruther until 1840, when he went to Edinburgh to become Conservator of the Museum of the College of Surgeons, then professor of anatomy 1846-67. He was famous for his study of cytology. He wrote many papers, including those on the growth of teeth, and on 'Centres of Nutrition'. His *Anatomical Memoirs* were issued in 1868. An eminent German pathologist, Rudolph Virchow, dedicated his *Cellular Pathology* to John Goodsir in 1859.

The Goodsir family - originally named Gutcher - were Huguenots who came to Fife from France in the seventeenth century . John was one of three surgeon sons of John Goodsir senior, who all followed the family tradition of medicine. With his younger brother, Henry, John showed a boyhood interest in anatomy; they would dissect and study the odd specimens that fishermen found in their nets. Henry, assistant surgeon, perished with the crew of *H.M.S. Erebus* on the ill fated Franklin expedition in search of the North West passage through the Arctic. Another brother, Robert, sailed in 1849 and again in 1850 in search of the expedition and his brother. John died in 1867, his health ruined by careless living.

John Goodsir senior purchased the site of the Hermitage - then a malt steading and barn from the Black family in 1814 for £210. He built the fine three storey house, which was completed in 1817. Later, in 1839, he purchased the adjoining cottage, hayloft and stable, known in James Melville's time as 'Baxter's Barn', which had been owned by a farming family from the mid-17th century.

The house remained in the Goodsir family until 1847, when it was bought by Thomas Black, surgeon. He was born in 1819 in East Wemyss, the son of a baker, and was encouraged to study medicine by a local doctor. He made two voyages to Greenland on a whaling vessel and was invited by "some influential gentlemen" to come to Anstruther and he took the place of Professor John Goodsir and of his lamented brother Henry. He was a Town Councillor and also for many years a keen horticulturist. In 1845 he married Jessie Phillips, niece of Archibald Williamson of Bellfield. Their eldest son, John, cashier and then partner of the firm Balfour Williamson, was a benefactor of Anstruther's Union Harbour and of Waid Academy. Robert, the second son, died at sea at the age of 19, and their surviving daughter, Elizabeth, as Mrs Logan, was a benefactor of the town and parish church.

At his death by drowning in Anstruther harbour at the age of 45 a monument in Anstruther churchyard was erected by public subscription.

The Blacks were followed by a succession of owners - James Cairns, veterinary surgeon , then Mrs Cairns, who called the house Rosebank, William Mitchell, shipmaster, Jane Erskine (1937) who gave the house its present name, The Hermitage, James Prain, jute manufacturer, Sandy Aitken, a building consultant, then in 1991 Mrs Margaret McDonald, who extensively restored the cottage section of the house.

BELLFIELD and the WILLIAMSONS / 6

The handsome and substantial house in School Green, Bellfield, was built in the late 1830s by Archibald Williamson, shipmaster and shipowner. The Williamsons were an old Kilrenny family. Archibald, the fourth surviving son of Stephen Williamson, farmer, maltster, and shipowner was born in 1757 in Cellardyke. He served his apprenticeship on one of his father's ships, the *Barbara and Mary* (Barbara was his youngest sister and Mary was his mother, Mary Grieve). Archibald inherited considerable shipping interests on the death of his father in 1813. He gave up an active career at sea when he married Isabella Lawson from Kettle in 1826. She was the sister of Alexander Lawson, linen manufacturer in Kingskettle, whose financial help enabled her son Stephen to set up, with Alexander Balfour from Leven the firm of Balfour Williamson, Liverpool.

Shortly after the birth of their son Stephen in 1827 in Cellardyke the family moved to Anstruther Wester to Marsfield House (now Anstruther Golf Club) and remained there for about ten years until Bellfield was built. In 1815 Archibald Williamson was admitted a member of the Anstruther Easter Sea Box Society, a seamans' charitable association and in 1838 was elected Boxmaster. His death in 1847 was much regretted by the managers of the Society "from the long and constant attention he paid to its interest".

Isabella continued to live at Bellfield until her death in February 1882 at the age of seventy nine. For some years she had been a member of the United Presbyterian Church in the Back Dykes but after her death her son Stephen, a member of the Free Church, gave Bellfield to the Chalmers' Memorial Church for a manse.

Bellfield House

13

Anstruther Easter's burgh school had been moved from "the dingy ben-end at the Tolbooth" up to the more salubrious Green in 1719. John Martin, a teacher in Liff where he was born in 1701, came as an assistant schoolmaster in 1727 and in 1734 was appointed schoolmaster. His rigorous teaching of Latin raised the reputation of Anster's school throughout the district, in spite of his complaint that his Latin class was beguiled from their *lesson by sparrows hopping out and in by the holes in the thatch.* He married twice, first Alison Simon, daughter of David Simon, writer and town clerk of Anstruther Easter, and secondly Mary Boyack from Dundee, mother of David, the artist, the fifth of John's nine children. John died of a fever in November 1772 and was buried in the parish churchyard. The schoolhouse must have been rebuilt in the late 19th century but the old school building survives in Murray & Wilson's joinery business.

At an early age David Martin showed a remarkable talent for drawing, particularly "bees, boats and horses". He studied under Allan Ramsey in Rome and in 1759, at the age of twenty-two, won first prize in the Royal Society of Arts competition with a black and white chalk drawing entitled *Antique Nude* which was much admired when exhibited by the R S A.

Returning from Italy he studied at the St Martin's Lane Academy and was appointed principal draughtsman and designer in Ramsey's studio. He worked with Ramsey for twenty years from 1752.

**School House
School Green**

He established his own studio in Edinburgh and dominated the portrait market there. In recognition of his success he was appointed Limner of the Prince of Wales (Royal portrait painter) in Scotland.

During the 1770s Martin painted more than three hundred portraits including those of the great lawyer Lord Mansfield, the philosopher David Hume, the chemists Joseph Black and William Cullen, Jean Jacques Rousseau and Thomas Carlyle as well as two self-portraits. He also made distinguished engravings of his own work. His finest and most famous portrait is that of the American statesman and scientist Benjamin Franklin, which hangs in the White House in Washington.

When the Kilrenny and Anstruther Burgh Collection discovered this fact contact was made with the White House through the Internet. They found David Martin's connection with Anstruther to be very interesting. The Burgh Collection was subsequently delighted to receive an excellent colour reproduction of the Franklin portrait which was e-mailed from the White House. Franklin sits at his desk beside a bust of Sir Isaac Newton.

Martin was a precursor of Henry Raeburn (born 1756) whose master, a goldsmith, encouraged his early efforts in paint and took him to see Martin's portraits in his studio in St James Square. There is a tenuous link with another Fife painter, David Wilkie (born 1785), who was given Martin's lay figures by Martin's brother, the Revd Samuel Martin, minister in Monimail, who was co-presbyter of Wilkie's father.

Works by Martin hang in the Scottish Portrait Gallery, the Royal Scottish Academy, St Andrews University, Paxton House Berwickshire, the Aberdeen Art Gallery, the City of Dundee Art Gallery, Kelvingrove and Scone Palace. The Scottish Academy held an exhibition of his work in 1937 and a recent one was held in the Crawford Centre, St Andrews in the autumn of 1997. This was undertaken by Lucy Dixon, who selected the exhibits and compiled the supporting catalogue. Her thorough research into Martin's career has resulted in an enormous increase in the number of paintings now attributed to the artist.

The artist died in 1797 and was buried in the parish of South Leith. Today the Burgh Collection is trying to trace the site of his unmarked grave and to erect a commemorative stone there to one of Anstruther's illustrious sons. The Burgh Collection is most grateful to Dr Barbara Anderson, a direct descendant of David Martin's two brothers, for donating to the Collection much of her research into the life and works of David Martin, artist.

Until the mid-19th century there was very little protection for ships at seas in a storm, and no indication of outstanding rocks. The cargoes which ships lost in winter storms were picked up by pirates. Local people lit bonfires of lamps along the coast to indicate obstacles, but these went out quickly.

In 1786 the Northern Lighthouse Trust was established to provide better light indication for ships at sea. Robert Stevenson (1728-1850), a distinguished civil engineer, and grandfather of Robert Louis Stevenson, became engineer to the Scottish Lighthouse Board. He designed 20 lighthouses, inventing intermittent and flashing lights. Thomas Stevenson (1818-1887), Louis' (always pronounced Lewis) father, an engineer and meteorologist, became joint engineer to the Board of Scottish Lighthouses from 1853 to 1885. He also was responsible for various innovations in lighthouse design.

It was taken for granted that the young R.L.S. (1850-1894) would follow the family tradition of engineering. Although literature was already his great passion, in 1868 Louis dutifully agreed to watch his father's firm work on the harbour in Anstruther. (His father also designed the Isle of May and Anstruther harbour lighthouses.) After Anstruther, in 1869 Louis made a tour of the Orkneys and Shetland aboard the steam yacht of the Commissioners of Northern Lights and in 1870 he toured the Western Isles, first staying on the Isle of Erraid - afterwards the setting used in the tale *Kidnapped*.

In Anstruther Louis stayed in Cunzie House, on the Crail Road, opposite the church. He lodged with Baillie Brown, a carpenter by trade.

Cunzie House

Stevenson enjoyed the scenery and environment in Anstruther, writing later that he even loved the place "for the sake of the sunshine, the thrilling seaside air, the wash of the waves on the sea-face, the green glimmer of divers' helmets far below, the musical clinking of the masons . . ." He spent his evenings composing stories and verses in his lodgings in Cunzie House, which he told his father "were very nice and I don't think there are any children. There is a box of mignonette in the window and a factor of dried rose-leaves which make the atmosphere a trifle heavy but very pleasant". He was already committed to becoming a writer. He had suffered poor health with respiratory problems since childhood - he did not go to school till he was nine. His fragile health and lack of interest persuaded Louis' father to let him change from studying engineering to law. He qualified as an advocate in 1875 but never practised.

About this time young Louis had a severe attack of tuberculosis. Looking for a warmer climate he went south across the channel to Paris. Here he met an American woman, Fanny Osborne. Separated from her husband, she had come to Paris to study art. Louis was smitten by this strong-minded independent woman. After she obtained a divorce he followed her to San Francisco where they were married in1880. Soon after they returned to Edinburgh for Fanny to meet Louis' parents. The visit was a great success, but Louis developed tuberculosis again. With his wife and step-children he moved to Switzerland, then San Francisco where Stevenson wrote *Treasure Island*. The story made Louis famous and put his finances on a stable footing. In 1888 he chartered a yacht to sail to the South Pacific, where he lived outside Apia, the capital of Samoa. He became a much loved friend and advocate of the local people. There in 1894 he died from an unexpected brain haemorrhage.

A stone plaque on the side of Cunzie House commemorates his stay in Anstruther in a verse quoted from his own poetry -

> *Not one quick beat of your warm heart*
> *Nor thought that came to you apart*
> *Pleasure nor pity, love nor pain*
> *Nor sorrow has gone by in vain.*

ANSTRUTHER

CELLARDYKE

ROBERT FOWLER, R C A , R I / 8

Anstruther Easter has its famous artist, born in School Green in 1737. Cellardyke also has its artist, not perhaps as widely known but of some standing in the late Victorian art world. The young Robert often visited his aunt Catherine Deas, wife of John Brown, cabinet-maker, at Cunzie House after the family had moved to Liverpool.

The Fowler family is an old one, the name appearing among magistrates in the earliest Kilrenny records. Some were mariners and shipmasters, others popular grocers in Cellardyke; one branch of the family set up a successful business in Australia and another did so in America.

Robert Fowler, baptised in Kilrenny church in May 1850, was the eldest son of Jessie Deas and Robert Fowler, shipmaster. His brother and five sisters were all born and baptised in Anstruther Easter, the youngest in 1863. Sometime before then the family had moved to Liverpool where his shipmaster father was "a pioneer sea captain" for Stephen Williamson of the firm Balfour Williamson, who seems to have made a point of employing natives of Cellardyke and Anstruther.

He was educated at the Liverpool Collegiate School, and on leaving he was apprenticed to an architect though his own inclination was to study art. He soon began to attend classes at the Royal Academy schools in London and also Heatherley's Art School where he "sought and found instruction and sympathy".

Until 1902 Robert lived and worked in Liverpool where his studio in West Derby was a centre of artistic life, not only for painters but for singers and musicians. He loved music and although he did not play himself he had a piano in the outer room for the benefit of musicians, who were always welcome in his studio.

He exhibited regularly in Liverpool where his work was highly appreciated and from 1876 in London at the Royal Academy and other galleries. He also exhibited in Paris, Brussels and Venice. He had a considerable reputation in Germany and was especially popular in Munich.

Robert Fowler RSW

18

The Royal Institute of Painters in Water Colours elected Fowler a member in 1891 and he was an associate of the Royal Cambrian Academy. He began painting mythological subjects in watercolour, *The coming of Apollo* exhibited at the Academy in 1896 being probably his most famous picture. Later he turned to landscapes in oils, one of which, *Windsor Castle*, was part of the Logan bequest to Anstruther in 1926. He was influenced by Japanese art, many examples of which decorated the home of his parents, and he was also a successful designer of striking posters.

Robert Fowler married and had two children, a son and a daughter. He died at New Ferry in the Wirral on the 28th October 1926 and like his parents was buried at West Derby. Liverpool's Walker Art Gallery owns several of his pictures and in the spring of 1927 held a memorial exhibition of his work.

A study by Robert Fowler

In 1768 a land labourer, William Tennant, bought a house at the east end of a remarkably narrow road, the High Street or Gait, Anstruther's main thoroughfare; there must have been great difficulty for passing horse drawn traffic.

The house was inherited by the eldest son, Alexander Tennant, a merchant and farmer, who rebuilt the house with two storeys in 1801. Alexander and his wife, Ann Watson of Cellardyke, had three sons and at least one daughter. The second of these sons, William, was born in 1784. Crippled at an early age, possibly by polio, he always walked with the help of crutches. At the burgh school he displayed a special gift for languages. His father decided that he should be a teacher, so at the age of fifteen he went to St Andrews University where he made rapid progress in Greek and Latin. Financial hardship brought by poor harvests in 1799 and 1800 meant that his father could no longer support him as a student, and he had to leave in 1801 without a degree.

Tennant continued his studies at home and in 1803 became clerk to his elder brother, Alexander, a corn factor in Glasgow. After two years the business was transferred to Anstruther, William returning to the house in the High Street where he worked at the poem that made him famous. In 1811 the business failed. Alexander absconded while creditors put William in the Debtor's room in West Anster. However, it was clear that he bore no responsibility for the firm's debts and he was released the next day. That was the end of William's commercial career.

Tennant had continued his studies of the classics during his eight years as a clerk and had also begun the study of Hebrew. In addition he had made his father's house a centre of literary activity in a remarkable club. The Dictionary of National Biography says that "..at the Anstruther Musomanik Society members assembled to enjoy the coruscations of their own festive minds", and that these members "..of the better class in town met there for mutual improvement and recreation". One of the more eminent members from outside Anstruther, Sir Walter Scott, was admitted to the society in 1815.

Tennant's literary aspirations were expressed in verse from an early age. His best known work, *Anster Fair*, published in 1812, is a poetical account of a country fair, based on the traditional Scottish ballad *Maggie Lauder*, imagined as taking place in the early sixteenth century in the presence of James V and his entourage. *Anster Fair* is a comic epic of 3544 lines set in six cantos.

> *What time from east, from west, from south, from north,*
> *From every hamlet, town, and smoky city,*
> *Laird, clown, and beau, to Anster Fair, came forth,*
> *The young, the gay, the handsome and the witty,*
> *To try in various sport and game their worth,*
> *Whilst prize before them MAGGIE sat, the pretty..*

A favourable notice written by Francis Jeffrey in *The Edinburgh Review* on the publication of the second edition brought acclaim and also acceptance of the author by the literary elite of Edinburgh.

After the publication of *Anster Fair* Tennant's academic career was reborn. He was appointed schoolmaster in Dunino, an inland parish between Anstruther and St Andrews. While there he improved his Hebrew scholarship and gained knowledge of Arabic, Syrian and Persian.

In 1816 he moved to a bigger school in Lasswade, the village in which his literary hero Sir Walter Scott had spent the first years of his married life. Students found him amiable and unselfish, fond of nature and innocent enjoyment. Never physically prepossessing - ". . . you see the professor swinging on his crutches . . . his hat is tied by a ribbon under his chin, and his happy face is rosy . . ." He was described as ". . . a mere apology for a man but every inch a gentleman".

In 1819 he was invited by the trustees of the newly founded Dollar Academy to teach classical and oriental languages. This marked an improvement in his financial position. He always practised strict domestic economy and was able to have a small villa built, "Devongrove", which he made his home for the rest of his life. As he was a bachelor his sister took charge of his domestic affairs.

In 1834 Tennant's old friend Francis Jeffrey, now Lord Advocate, appointed him to the chair of oriental languages in St Mary's College at the University of St Andrews.

Poor health forced Professor Tennant to relinquish his chair and he died at Devongrove in October 1848. Soon after his death a number of his friends and townsmen erected a monument to his memory in Anstruther churchyard. It consists of a handsome obelisk of polished freestone, about 11 feet high. It bears a Latin inscription, in translation:

Here lies interred
William Tennant, Doctor of Laws
Professor of Oriental Languages in St Mary's College, St Andrews
A man of great mental endowments
And of varied and profound learning
Beloved for his benevolence and urbanity
He was a skilful,sweet and humorous poet
Born in this town, of a respectable family and educated in the
College of St Salvator and St Leonard, at St Andrews . . . .

There is a also a plaque recording the past presence and celebrity of William Tennant on the wall of 54-56 High Street, now a pet shop, "Pets Pantry".

DAVID MURRAY and the MURRAY LIBRARY / 10

Fife County Library Services did not come into existence until November 1921, but Anstruther was fortunate in having the public-spirited David Murray to give the town a library, which is named after him.

The Murray Library Trustees, formally established on 10th June 1908, were to consist of representatives of the community of Anstruther Easter. At the beginning it was decided that it was desirable for the purpose of attracting to the said library and reading room the young men of the community "that recreation rooms should be an adjunct" and the trustees decided to "place therein billiard tables and other recreative apparatus". On July 5th they announced that they had been successful in purchasing two adjacent sites on Shore Street "with a superb view of the Firth of Forth". Two "Imperial" billiard tables were built by Gray and Pringle of Anstruther, and the tiles in the lobby and the mosaic in the vestibule were the work of Messrs Howdon of Edinburgh. No expense was spared.

A book endowment fund was started to which David Murray's brother, William, and sister, Mrs Helen Pittendrigh, donated £1,000. The trustees wished to make it clear that it was as near a "Free Library" as possible and the annual subscription was fixed at 3 shillings a year and 5 shillings if billiards was included.

The great and good were assembled for the Grand Opening on 30th December 1908: the local MP, Major Anstruther-Gray, Sir Ralph and Lady Anstruther, and representatives of the Carnegie Trust, Dunfermline, and the Carnegie Library, Edinburgh and no fewer than six ministers.

The opening was performed by Mrs Henry Watson, niece of David Murray (her daughter, Miss Helen Watson, still cherishes the silver key). Sir Ralph Anstruther, the *East of Fife Record* reported, congratulated the trustees on their stalwart work and declared that he was a great believer in good, sound fiction as an educational force, "particularly fiction which described life as it really was and not merely the imagination and theories of the author (applause)." Dr Ross of the Carnegie Trust spoke of the reading and billiard rooms which besides providing recreation "were good moralising agents, drawing young men from the public house and providing them with legitimate occupation for their leisure hours (applause)". A splendid tea was provided for the large company by Mrs Pittendrigh.

David Murray, merchant, of London and Adelaide, was born in Anstruther, the eldest son of William Murray, draper, a popular provost of Anstruther. David was educated at the burgh school and Madras College, St Andrews. In 1853, still in their twenties, he and his brother William having served their apprenticeships with their father and gained further experience in Glasgow, set off like many enterprising Scots at that time to make a new life in Australia. They settled in Adelaide and started a drapery business which eventually became "one of the best and most profitable in Australia" and one of the largest employers in the Commonwealth with branches in Perth, Melbourne, Sydney and Broken Hill.

In 1870 David Murray "to discharge his social and civic duties" entered Parliament as Representative for East Adelaide. In 1882 he became a Member of the Legislative Council and Chief Secretary to the government. He was described as "saying what he meant in clear, terse language, and of ending his speeches when he had said all that was necessary". He was an Elder of the Kirk and President of the YMCA in Adelaide, member of the Council of Adelaide University and a generous benefactor of good causes.

In his later years he paid frequent visits to Anstruther with his wife Rebecca from his residence in London's fashionable Bayswater. He died in London in January 1907 leaving in his will £4,000 to provide a library and reading room in his home town: he had always loved books and had his own large and varied library. David Murray was buried, as he had wished, in Anstruther churchyard and it is touchingly recorded that "out of respect" the shops on the route to the churchyard were closed for two hours.

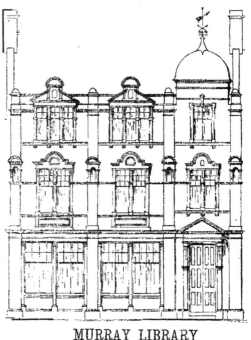

MURRAY LIBRARY

In 1997 there was unveiled in the Crown Court Church of Scotland, Covent Garden, London, a stained glass window dedicated to the memory of a man born and brought up in Anstruther. The window, the last of several portraits of Scottish historical figures, was of Thomas Chalmers, born in 1780 in a house in what is now Post Office Close.

This house at the back of the Close is one of the oldest in Anstruther. In 1560 it was occupied by the first Protestant minister of Anstruther Wester Church. It was then a three-storeyed house at the foot of the slope from the High Street. In 1707 the old house was bought and restored by Philip Brown, shipmaster, who raised the old "close and yaird" to its present level so that the ground floor of the old building is now a cellar. After standing for many years in a state of disrepair the house was fully restored in 1981 by the well known joiner and builder Peter Murray. In 1991 Mr Murray carried out further restoration work on the attic and cellars.

Thomas Chalmers' Birthplace

Of Philip Brown's four great grandsons, Paton or Patton, who were born in this house in the early 18th century, one became an admiral in the Royal Navy, another a captain in charge of naval transport at Portsmouth during the Napoleonic wars and a third military secretary to the governor-general of India and later governor of St Helena. The fourth died as a young man in Calcutta while in the service of the East India Company.

Thomas Chalmers was born in the box-bed in the room to the left of the front door on March 17th 1780. His father was at the time building his "new house above the mill" where Thomas spent his childhood. Old Post Office Close took its name from the post office which was established in the little room to the right of the front door in the early 1840s until it was moved to the High Street in 1851.

Thomas Chalmers was the sixth child of a family of fourteen born to John Chalmers, dyer, general merchant and provost of Anstruther, and his wife Elizabeth Hall, daughter of a Crail wine merchant. He attended the burgh school and was admitted to St Andrews University before he was twelve (not unusual in those days) and referred to his first year there as a "mental Elysium". He showed an aptitude for mathematics and his ambition at this stage was to become a professor of mathematics.

His parents, however, wished him to become a minister and in 1803 he was called to Kilmany Church. He admitted that it was the nearness of St Andrews that attracted him to this charge for it was still his ambition to obtain a chair in mathematics there, but the untimely deaths of a dear sister and brother affected him deeply. He also suffered a serious debilitating illness and on his recovery decided to dedicate his life to the church. He became an inspired preacher and "Kilmany Church and Manse became the centre of a mighty spiritual influence".

In 1815 as a result of his now widespread reputation Chalmers went to the Tron Church, Glasgow. People travelled from all over the country to hear the great preacher, many spending the night in Glasgow to travel home the next day . In 1817 he was invited to London to meet many famous statesmen and leading literary figures. "All the world has gone wild about Chalmers". William Wilberforce, the anti-slavery campaigner, became a close friend. "Chalmers spoke with prophetic fury " wrote the essayist and critic William Hazlitt.

On his return to Glasgow Chalmers embarked on his scheme for elders and members of his congregation to go into the community and organise practical help for the needy and helpless. This additional burden exhausted Chalmers and in 1824 he accepted the chair of moral philosophy at St Andrews University and shortly afterwards the chair of divinity at Edinburgh.

For many years there had been growing discontent with the government of the Church of Scotland. One crucial question was who should appoint the minister, the patron of the living or the congregation.

Thomas Chalmers took the lead in resolving the dispute in favour of the congregation and the independence of the Church. On the grey morning of the 18th May 1843 at the Church of Scotland's General Assembly in Edinburgh some four hundred ministers quietly rose from their seats and in orderly fashion filed out of the building and out of the Church. Thousands gathered to cheer them through the streets to Tanfield where, after the signing of the Deed of Demission, the Free Church was born with Chalmers as its first Moderator.

The four hundred were evicted from their churches and manses practically overnight and would have suffered even greater hardship but for Chalmers' forethought. In 1842 when disruption seemed inevitable Chalmers provided a plan of financial support, his Sustenation Fund, without which the Free Church would never have survived. Within three years of the Disruption Chalmers and the new congregations raised funds to build numerous churches, manses and schools and 3 Theological Colleges. "The money", said Chalmers, "has come in like rain".

In May 1847 Thomas Chalmers travelled to London to address members of the House of Commons on the progress of the Free Church. He returned to Edinburgh to address the Free Church Assembly but died that night peacefully in his sleep at the age of sixty seven. His funeral was the largest ever seen in Edinburgh. He was a well-loved and venerated figure and "by common consent the most illustrious Scot of his time". So ended the life of one of Scotland's and Anstruther's most famous sons.

Chalmers' House

The Chalmers family moved to the house now known as Chalmers' House when Thomas was a young boy.

Wightman's Wynd

Throughout the 17th and 18th centuries Anstruther and the Isle of May had a long history of smuggling to evade excise duties. After the 1707 Act of Union heavy taxes were imposed on salt, malt and any commodities containing either of them. This led to a serious decline in Scottish trade and encouraged smuggling.

Besides goods, after the "Glorious Revolution" of 1688 smuggling extended to helping Jacobites - supporters of the old Stuart dynasty. The Fife lairds supported the 1715 and 1745 Jacobite risings. Thomas Auchinleck, who was minister for a short time in Anstruther Wester, supported the Jacobites and, it was claimed, was an Episcopalian at heart.

In 1715, disguised under the name of Maule, the Earl of Mar arrived at Elie from London in a coaling ship and then made his way to Kilrenny, where Sir Alexander Erskine of Cambo joined him. Together they went north to recruit troops, returning to Fife with about 2000 men. The Master of Sinclair led another party from St Andrews. Under the command of William MacIntosh of Borlum the troops embarked in small boats along the East Neuk, and were ferried to North Berwick. The Jacobites captured Edinburgh, but after this first success the rising was put down. In 1745 Prince Charles Stuart led the second Jacobite rising.

In Anstruther a merchant and smuggler, Charles Wightman, who lived in a house next to the site of Dreel Castle, provided a safe refuge for the defeated clansman after the Battle of Culloden. Through his smuggling connections he arranged safe passages for them to France. The house no longer exists, but the little lane alongside the ruins of Dreel Castle is called Wightman's Wynd. The square tower at the foot of the Wynd and the wall with a "dumb-bell' loophole, both dating from the 16th century, were part of Wightman's house, which he bought in 1749.

There is evidence that Anstruther Wester gave the Jacobites some material support. The old town council owned a letter from one Murray of Broughton, "Treasurer" for Prince Charles, excusing Anstruther Wester from paying excise duties for six months in thanks for their contribution to the Jacobite cause. Of course the citizens were unable to benefit from this beneficence. The letter is now lodged in the archives of the library of the University of St Andrews.

The White House overlooks the harbour of Anstruther Wester. Early in the seventeenth century William Darsie, merchant and sea captain, had a house on this site. The present house with its Dutch gable, once nicknamed "Sir Harry's Fort", was built in 1760 by Sir Henry Erskine who became member of Parliament for the East of Fife Burghs in 1753, displacing General Sir Philip Anstruther. David Hume wrote that Sir Harry had "made an attack on the General's Burghs and by the assistance of his uncle's (General Sinclair) interest and purse is likely to prevail". Bad blood between Sir Harry and Sir Philip had originated in Minorca where Sir Harry had been arrested and confined for three weeks by the General without any charge. In revenge Erskine had displaced Anstruther from his parliamentary seat.

Perhaps Sir Harry saw encouragement of the local economy as a part of his obligations as member of parliament. He was responsible for setting up a Brussels carpet weaver and his sons in a business in Pittenweem. There is a note in the minutes of the Anstruther Town Council for 26th June 1765: "Mr Johnstone, senior, having made a present to the town of a rich carpet, made at Sir Harry Erskine's factory at Pittenweem, for an ornament to the magistrates left in Anstruther Kirk, the Council accept thereof, and return to him their hearty thanks for this testimony of his regard for the community."

Sir Harry married Janet, sister of Alexander Wedderburn, later Lord Chancellor and 1st Earl of Rosslyn, and had two sons and a daughter, the elder son becoming 2nd Earl Rosslyn. Erskine resigned his parliamentary seat in May 1765 on his appointment as secretary of the Most Ancient and Noble Order of the Thistle. He died at York in August of that year while on his way to his new home in Kew.

In the mid-19th century the White House was the residence of an elderly lady and her daughter. The younger lady was Margaret Oliphant, a prolific and popular author. Some of her novels are set in Anstruther. From *Katie Stewart*:"The little town of Anstruther stands on the side of the Firth . . . A row of houses, straggling here and there into corners, turn their faces to the harbour. This is called the Shore . . . there have been great people here - Maggie Lauder, Professor Tennant, Dr Chalmers. The world has heard of the quiet burghs of East and West Anster."

Margaret Oliphant Wilson (1828-97) married her cousin Francis Wilson Oliphant, a painter and designer who worked with Pugin on windows in the Houses of Parliament and designed windows for Ely Cathedral and Kings College, Cambridge. He died young, leaving Mrs Oliphant to bring up her two sons alone. She also took responsibility for her brother's children when he died. This caused her financial difficulties in spite of her many published works. She wrote almost a hundred novels, scholarly works on Cervantes and Dante and stories in Blackwood's Magazine. As a lifelong friend of that the publisher, Blackwood, she wrote two volumes of a biographical account of his family.

A solicitor, Henry Watson, bought the house and adjacent properties in 1909 on behalf of Louisa Murray, his cousin by marriage. David Murray and his brother William, father of Louisa, had established a successful business in Australia, and gave money to build the Murray Library in Shore Street. On her death in1962 the White House was bought by the National Trust for Scotland who in 1965 sold it with a Deed of Conditions for the preservation of the historic house to a restoring purchaser, Dr Mackintosh, a pioneer of the micro-electronics industry in Fife. The house is now owned by a retired architect.

The White House, on the corner of The Esplanade

John Keay was born in East Green in September 1828. He was of sea-faring ancestry, his father being Captain Thomas Keay, master of the brig *Medium* of Anstruther. As a matter of course when schooldays were completed the son followed his father's calling and under his father served his sea apprenticeship. Later he sailed with Captain Robert Fowler of Cellardyke, father of the artist, who is described as a fine seaman and a man of sterling Christian character by the young men who sailed with him, all of whom revered him as a commander and as a man. Under the incentive of such examples as those of his father and Captain Fowler were developed those qualities which characterised Captain Keay throughout his strenuous career.

Very quickly John Keay climbed the ladder of promotion and at an early age was in command of the *Ellen Rodger* belonging to Captain Rodger of Cellardyke. He sailed the seven seas and with his experience and seamanship became one of that select band of masters of the China tea clippers of the late 60s and early 70s. In 1859 commanding the *Ellen Rodger*, reputed to be one of the fastest ships ever in the China trade, he arrived home first in the race from China to London with the season's first cargo of tea and in 1860 and 61 he was second and third home. In 1862 and 63 he was captain of the *Falcon* and third on each occasion and in 64 was eighth.

Captain Rodger's *Ariel* was launched in 1865 and Captain Keay commanded her for 3 years. 1866 was the year of the famous dead heat with *Taeping*; in 1867 *Ariel* was third home *Taeping* being first; in 1868 Captain Keay was first home in *Ariel*; the last time he commanded a sailing ship.

With the opening of the Suez Canal in 1869 Captain Keay transferred to steam and in 1874 was first home with the season's first cargo of tea in the steamer *Glencartney* 86 days out of Yokohama. He spent a number of useful years in several well-known shipping lines with much acceptance to his owners and an ever increasing esteem in maritime circles.

John Keay married Helen Dishington, second daughter of George Dishington and Ann Roger "daughter of a sailor in Kilrenny" and in 1869 bought his father-in-law's house in West Anstruther, *Fernbank*, across from the Buckie House. Only one of his three surviving sons went to sea. One who did not, Robert Dishington Keay, born in 1869, was an engineer. Educated at Liverpool College he distinguished himself in athletics and was head boy of the school.

Fernbank

He was largely responsible for the building of the great Scotstown works in Glasgow and in 1914 was sent to Esquimault, Vancouver Island, as manager of a shipyard for Yarrows Ltd, with whom he had worked for twenty years. He died in Victoria two years later at the early age of 49.

John Keay was appointed manager of a steamship line in Liverpool towards the end of his life and left Anstruther where up to that time he had made his home at *Fernbank* (now known as *The Great Lodging*).

In Liverpool, even after retirement, Captain Keay was associated with many philanthropic and other institutions connected with sea-faring; the Seamans' Hospital, the Merchant Marine Service Association, the Home for Aged Mariners and the Seamans' Orphanage. He was also a director of HMS Training Ship *Conway.* He died at Anfield Road, Liverpool, in March 1918 in his 90th year.

The Buckie House was built in 1692. A map of 1790 shows that it was next to a market, with a market cross which has now gone. The house was later decorated with shells by Alexander Batchelor, a slater and joiner who was described as "a somewhat odd and ingenious character - a capital tradesman in his prime days".

Buckie House

The grotto room ceiling, still extant, is his masterpiece under which he displayed a coffin that he designed for himself and which was also heavily enshelled. The report of his death in the *East of Fife Record* of 13th April 1866 included the suggestion that the coffin should be preserved for posterity. However it has not been seen since that date so it must be assumed that Alexander Batchelor's last wishes were respected.

The "celebrated shell house" was fondly recalled by Robert Louis Stevenson writing some years after his visit to the town in 1868. Unfortunately it is something of a hazard to modern traffic as it stands at a dramatic left-hand turn into Elizabeth Place on the road from Pittenweem. The town council brought forward several schemes to ease the traffic problems over the years, and there was even talk of demolishing the Buckie House. Fortunately the National Trust for Scotland came to the rescue, purchasing the Buckie House and the adjoining smaller property, a two-storey house that has its entrance on West Anstruther High Street. This housed a second-hand furniture shop in the 1940s, "Ruth's Economic Store". The Trust restored the external shell decoration of the Buckie House and also its most remarkable feature, the Grotto Room on the first floor with its elaborate ceiling of shells arranged in a classical design. The two properties were then sold together to the artist Derek Thirkell, who turned the ground floor of the smaller house into the Buckie House Gallery, where his own and other artists' work were displayed and sold.

SOURCES AND REFERENCES

Anson, Peter : *Fisher Boats and Fisher Folk on the East Coast of Scotland*, London 1930
Archives Department, University of St Andrews Library, North Street, St Andrews
Bathurst, Bella: *The Lighthouse Stevensons*, Harper Collins 1999
Conolly, Matthew: *Eminent Men of Fife*, published c.1880
David Murray's Trustees, Excerpts, Trustees of the Murray Library
(thanks to Mr Brian Minto)
Dictionary of National Biography, Oxford University Press
East of Fife Record
Eunson, Eric: *Old Anstruther in Photographs*, Stenlake Publishing,
Ochiltree, Ayrshire 1997
Glen, Duncan: *Illustrious Fife*, AKROS, Kirkcaldy 1998
Gourlay, George: *Anstruther: or Illustrations of Scottish Burgh Life* 1888
Gourlay, George: *Our Old Neighbours or Folklore of the East of Fife* 1887
Jope Slade: *A Man of Liverpool and his Art*, in STUDIO 9 pp 85-98, 1897
Lubbock, Basil:*The China Clippers*
McEwan, Peter J.M.: *Dictionary of Scottish Art and Architecture*,
Antique Collectors Club 1994
MacGregor, Forbes: *Salt Sprayed Burgh*, Pine Tree Press, Edinburgh EH12 6JS 1994
Murray Library Trustees, *Minute Book*
A Pictish Trail through the East Neuk of Fife,
East Neuk Churches Joint Consultative Group 1998
Statistical Account of Scotland 1791-98 Vol. 111 Anstruther
Statistical Account of Scotland 1845 Vol. 1X Anstruther
Stevenson, Stephanie: *A History of Anstruther*, John Donald 1989
Stevenson, Stephanie: *Chalmers' Birthplace*,
Anstruther Improvements Association 1983
Stevenson, Stephanie: *An Historic Walk Around Anstruther*,
Anstruther Improvements Association 1984
Tennant, William: *Anster Fair*, edition John Ross, Edinburgh 1871
Thirkell, Alison: *Auld Anster*, Buckie House Gallery
Watson, Harry: *Kilrenny and Cellardyke*, John Donald 1986